GRENOBLE
TRAVEL GUIDE
2024

Grenoble Unlocked: Your Gateway to French Alps Adventure

Philip Mablood

Copyright 2024, Philip Mablood.
All Rights Reserved!
No part of this book may be reproduced, stored in a retrieval system, or transmitted in any form or by any means, electronic, mechanical, photocopying, recording, or otherwise, without written permission of the copyright owner.

TABLE OF CONTENTS

Introduction
- Welcome to Grenoble
- What Makes Grenoble Unique
- How to Use This Guide

Getting to Know Grenoble
- History of Grenoble
- Geography and Climate
- Culture and Cuisine

Exploring the City
- Old Town: A Stroll Through History
- Bastille: Iconic Landmark Overlooking the City
- Museums and Galleries
- Culinary Delights: Where to Eat and Drink

Outdoor Adventures
- Hiking in the French Alps
- Skiing and Snowboarding
- Cycling Routes Around Grenoble
- Paragliding and Other Airborne Activities

Day Trips and Excursions
- Chartreuse Mountains: A Day in Nature
- Vercors Regional Natural Park
- Annecy: The Venice of the Alps

Nightlife and Entertainment
- Bars and Cafes
- Performing Arts and Music Scene
- Nighttime Views and Activities

Practical Information

Transportation in Grenoble

Accommodation Options

Safety Tips and Emergency Contacts

Useful Phrases in French

Additional Resources

Further Reading and Websites

Maps and Apps for Exploring Grenoble

Tourist Information Centers

Conclusion

Saying Goodbye to Thailand Grenoble

Introduction

Welcome to Grenoble

Welcome to Grenoble: Where Nature and Innovation Converge

Grenoble, which lies tucked away at the base of the French Alps, entices with its singular fusion of breathtaking scenery, extensive history, and cutting-edge innovation. This energetic city will attract you as soon as you arrive with its beautiful scenery, lively culture, and friendly people. Greetings from Grenoble, a city full of hidden gems waiting to be discovered around every turn.

A Glimpse into History

Grenoble's past is intertwined with the present, with a history spanning over two millennia. Originally established by the Gauls, it grew into an important Roman colony and then a prosperous medieval town. Grenoble has seen battles, revolutions, and triumphant moments over the ages, all of which have left their imprint on the cityscape.

Embracing Innovation

Grenoble, known as the "Capital of the Alps," is a historical city that is also at the forefront of innovation. The city serves as a center for scientific research and technical growth because of its top-notch academic institutes and thriving tech sector. The future is still being shaped by Grenoble's pioneering attitude, from nanotechnology to renewable energy.

A Feast for the Senses

Awaken your senses and get ready to discover Grenoble's gastronomic scene. The city is a gourmet haven, with everything from posh restaurants serving avant-garde food to little bistros providing traditional Alpine fare. Enjoy regional delicacies like raclette, dauphinois, and Chartreuse liqueur, and let each taste take you even farther into the heart of French cuisine.

Natural Splendor

Outdoor lovers have an endless playground all year round in Grenoble's magnificent surroundings. The adjacent ski resorts entice with their snowy slopes and thrilling descents come wintertime. Hikers, bikers, and environment enthusiasts are invited to discover the hidden gems that the verdant valleys and immaculate lakes have to offer in summertime. Whether you're looking for heart-pounding experiences or quiet times to yourself, Grenoble provides a haven in the breathtaking natural world.

Cultural Kaleidoscope

Explore the rich cultural landscape of Grenoble to see a mosaic of creative expression. The city takes great pride in its diversity, which ranges from top-notch museums exhibiting historical and artistic marvels to cutting-edge galleries stretching the frontiers of creation. Take in the passion and intensity of live music acts, dance festivals, and theatrical productions that liven up the streets.

Architectural Marvels

Grenoble's dynamic growth and rich past are reflected in its architectural environment. Explore the Old Town's cobblestone lanes, where historic structures silently pay respect to bygone times. Admire the opulence of Gothic cathedrals that evoke thoughts of bygone eras, as well as the graceful façades of Renaissance homes. You will discover new historical strata carved into Grenoble's walls with every step.

Breathtaking Views

Reach new heights and observe Grenoble from above, where expansive views provide a peek at the magnificence of the city. Take the well-known Grenoble Bastille cable car to the top to take in the expansive vistas of the Alps that go as far as the eye can see. Watch as the city comes to life beneath a blanket of stars, its sparkling lights casting an entrancing glow over the night sky.

A Warm Welcome Awaits

Grenoble's hospitality is a way of life, not just a custom. You will always be met with a friendly smile and sincere kindness, whether you are strolling around the city's narrow streets or enjoying an espresso at a sidewalk cafe. Spend some time getting to know the people, exchanging tales, and becoming fully enmeshed in the colorful fabric of Grenoble's society.

Your Grenoble Adventure Begins

Let wonder be your constant companion and curiosity your guide as you set out on your journey through Grenoble. Every moment holds the possibility of a brand-new adventure waiting to be discovered, from the snow-capped peaks of the Alps to the cobblestone lanes of the Old Town. Enjoy the flavors, take in the sights, and embrace the spirit of exploration that makes this amazing city what it is. Welcome to Grenoble, where each event is a work of art just waiting to be captured on film in your recollections.

What Makes Grenoble Unique

Grenoble is a distinctive travel destination for several strong reasons.

Alpine Setting: Grenoble is surrounded by breathtaking scenery because it is located at the base of the French Alps. Unmatched year-round outdoor activity options are provided by the area's closeness to the mountains, from hiking and biking in the summer to skiing and snowboarding in the winter.

Innovation Hub: Grenoble is renowned for its inventive spirit and is a top research and technology hub. Numerous research institutes, notably the esteemed Grenoble

Alpes University, are located in the city, encouraging innovations in fields including biotechnology, nanotechnology, and renewable energy.

Historical Significance: Grenoble's streets have more depth and personality because of its rich past. From its roots as a Roman town to its participation in the French Revolution, the city has been a witness to crucial periods in European history. Exploring Grenoble is like going back in time, with architectural marvels and cultural icons at every turn.

Cultural Diversity: Grenoble's lively cultural scene reflects its diversified population and foreign impact. The city invites individuals from all over the world, producing a melting pot of languages, cultures, and ideas. Visitors may enjoy this cultural diversity through festivals, art exhibitions, and gastronomic delicacies from throughout the globe.

Sustainable Lifestyle: Grenoble is devoted to sustainability and environmental management. With vast public transit networks, bike-friendly infrastructure, and attempts to minimize carbon emissions, the city is a model for eco-conscious urban life. Visitors may explore Grenoble with a free conscience, knowing that their footsteps tread softly on the globe.

Gastronomic Delights: French food takes center stage in Grenoble, with a special Alpine flair. Local delights like gratin dauphinois, raclette, and Chartreuse liquor tickle the taste buds, while lively markets and exquisite restaurants offer a feast for food connoisseurs. The great gastronomic legacy and inventiveness of Grenoble are reflected in its scene.

Gateway to Adventure: Grenoble, known as the "Capital of the Alps," is a starting point for outdoor exploration. The options are unlimited, whether you're looking for heart-pounding thrills or serene moments in the great outdoors. Grenoble has activities for all outdoor enthusiasts, from paragliding over stunning landscapes to skiing and snowboarding at world-class resorts.

Lively Urban Energy: Grenoble is a bustling urban center full of life, even if it is close to nature. Every element of the city, from bustling street markets to elegant boutiques and hip cafes, beckons investigation. There's always something fascinating going on in Grenoble thanks to its cultural events, live music venues, and nightlife offerings.

Grenoble is a place that captivates the imagination and makes a lasting impact on everyone who visits, owing to its unique blend of natural beauty, innovation, history, and culture.

How to Use This Guide

It's easy and uncomplicated to discover Grenoble using this guide. How to maximize it is as follows:

Navigate the Table of Contents: To gain a sense of what the handbook has to offer, start by looking at the table of contents. Every segment is intended to assist you in exploring many facets of Grenoble, ranging from its heritage and customs to outdoor pursuits and useful guidance.

Set Your Priorities: Choose the parts of Grenoble you want to see first, based on your tastes and areas of interest. Do you find yourself drawn to the historical sites of the city, or are outdoor excursions more your style? Locate pertinent portions using the table of contents, then adjust your schedule appropriately.

Read Descriptions and Recommendations: Explore each area to get thorough explanations and suggestions for making the most of your time in Grenoble. Whether you want to go on outdoor adventures, sample local food, or visit museums, you'll discover insightful advice to make the most of your time.

Follow Insider Tips: Throughout the guide, some hints and recommendations should not be missed. These opinions, which are sourced from knowledgeable locals and frequent visitors, provide insightful guidance on undiscovered treasures, lesser-known places, and distinctive experiences that aren't included in standard travel books.

Use Practical Information: For important information on lodging, travel, safety, and helpful French words, see the practical information section. With the aid of this information, you will be able to easily navigate Grenoble and guarantee a seamless and pleasurable stay.

Keep an Open Mind: Although this tour offers a thorough overview of Grenoble, don't be scared to stray off the main route and find new things. Accept chance meetings, engage in conversation with locals, and permit yourself to fully experience the lively atmosphere and culture of the city.

Share Your Experience: Talk to others about your adventures in Grenoble once they've ended. Through social media, travel forums, or first-hand stories, you may share your wisdom and suggestions with other tourists, encouraging them to explore this fascinating city together.

You'll go on an unforgettable tour across Grenoble by following these instructions and utilizing this guide as your guide. You'll discover its hidden gems and get a sense of this enchanted place.

Getting to Know Grenoble

History of Grenoble

A Journey Through Time: The History of Grenoble

The history of Grenoble spans more than two millennia and is woven with strands of conquest, invention, and tenacity. The city has experienced numerous changes that have left their imprint on its identity and topography, from its modest origins as a settlement of Gallic settlers to its current position as a thriving center of culture and technology. Come along on a historical voyage with us as we reveal Grenoble's fascinating tale.

Ancient Origins

Grenoble's history started in antiquity, as there is proof of human habitation going back to the prehistoric era. But because of the area's advantageous location at the meeting point of the Isère and Drac rivers, the Gauls were the ones to settle there initially. This French village, called Cularo, flourished as a military stronghold and trading hub, establishing the groundwork for the eventual city.

Roman Conquest and Expansion

Grenoble came under Roman control when the Gaulish tribes in the area were subjugated by the Roman general Caius Marius in 121 BCE. The Romans laid the foundation for the growth of a thriving Roman town by establishing a military garrison in the region because they understood its strategic importance. With streets around temples, forums, and baths, Grenoble prospered as a hub of administration and trade under Roman control.

Medieval Splendor

With the collapse of the Roman Empire, Grenoble passed into the hands of different Germanic tribes until being integrated into the Kingdom of Burgundy in the 5th century CE. The medieval period saw Grenoble come to prominence as a provincial center under the reign of the Counts of Albon. The city became a center of trade and culture, its fortunes helped by its advantageous placement along the Alpine trade routes.

In the 13th century, Grenoble was granted a charter by the Dauphin, establishing it as a free city under the protection of the French crown. This increased autonomy fostered Grenoble's economic and cultural expansion, as craftsmen, merchants, and intellectuals came to the city, contributing to its affluence and prominence.

The French Revolution and Beyond

The French Revolution of 1789 brought enormous changes to Grenoble, as revolutionary enthusiasm swept across the city. In 1788, Grenoble became the scene of the legendary Day of the Tiles, a precursor to the revolution in which an angry populace rioted against royal authority. This event marked the beginning of Grenoble's active engagement in the revolutionary movement, as the city adopted the ideas of liberty, equality, and brotherhood.

Throughout the 19th and 20th centuries, Grenoble continued to adapt, experiencing phases of expansion, innovation, and instability. The Industrial Revolution brought wealth to the city, as textile mills, hydropower facilities, and metallurgical enterprises drove its economy. Grenoble has flourished as a center of study and culture, with the development of famous colleges and cultural organizations.

A Hub of Innovation

Grenoble cemented its standing as a hub of technological innovation throughout the 20th century. Because of the city's accessibility to the Alps and plenty of hydroelectric power, it became a magnet for engineers and scientists, resulting in the emergence of innovative enterprises and research organizations. With its pioneering work in physics, chemistry, and biotechnology, Grenoble gained the moniker "Capital of the Alps."

Grenoble is a living example of its vibrant energy and rich history today. Its medieval defenses combine with cutting-edge research centers, and its historic streets stand in stark contrast to contemporary skyscrapers. The city maintains its commitment to innovation and development while respecting its cultural legacy, resulting in a distinctive fusion of modernity and tradition that characterizes its identity.

Preserving the Past, Embracing the Future

Grenoble is dedicated to maintaining its history while seizing the potential of the future as it looks to the future. Grenoble's rich history is preserved through historic sites like the Bastille fortification and the Cathedral of Notre Dame, and the city will continue to thrive and adapt for many years to come thanks to programs that encourage sustainability and environmental responsibility.

Grenoble's history demonstrates the tenacity and flexibility of its citizens. Grenoble's history is one of tenacity, ingenuity, and advancement from its prehistoric beginnings to its current position as a center of innovation.

Geography and Climate

Geography: Where Mountains Meet the City

Grenoble's breathtaking location at the base of the French Alps is a feature of its topography, which makes it an appealing travel destination for both nature lovers and thrill seekers. Grenoble is a city in the Auvergne-Rhône-Alpes region of southeast France, tucked in between the Drac and Isère rivers.

Magnificent mountain ranges, including the Chartreuse, Vercors, and Belledonne massifs, around the city offer countless chances for outdoor adventure in addition to a stunning background. The distinctive combination of new construction and old architecture characterizes Grenoble's urban landscape, which is dominated by the landmark Bastille fortification built atop a hill overlooking the city.

Grenoble is divided into several neighborhoods by the Isère River, which also serves as a natural gathering place for recreational activities. The city's many areas are connected by bridges that cross the river and provide beautiful views of the surrounding mountains and the calm waters below.

Climate: Four Seasons of Alpine Beauty

Due to its closeness to the Alps, Grenoble has a varied climate with different seasons that highlight the area's year-round natural splendor.

Spring (March to May): As the city emerges from the winter cold, Grenoble has moderate weather and a beautiful floral display. Adventurers may partake in outdoor pursuits including hiking, cycling, and picnicking amidst the verdant surroundings of the neighboring parks and mountains.

Summer (June to August): With pleasant temperatures and extended daylight hours ideal for outdoor exploration, summer is Grenoble's busiest travel season. There are many experiences to be experienced, including bathing in alpine lakes and climbing in the Alps. Festivals, outdoor music performances, and cultural events bring the city to life and create a lively environment that appeals to both inhabitants and visitors.

Autumn (September to November): Grenoble's landscapes are changed by the vivid hues of fall leaves as temperatures start to drop. Travelers are encouraged to take strolls in the city's parks and gardens, go on picturesque drives, and sample wine in the neighboring vineyards due to the refreshing mountain air.

Winter (December to February): The surrounding mountains are transformed into a wintry paradise as a coating of snow envelops Grenoble. Ski destinations with world-class skiing, snowboarding, and other winter sports, such as Chamrousse, Les Deux Alpes, and Alpe d'Huez, are only a short drive away. During the winter months, back in the city, warm and entertaining activities such as holiday markets, heated cafés, and cultural events are available.

All things considered, Grenoble's climate and topography provide a wide range of experiences for visitors all year long, whether they are looking for outdoor pursuits in the Alps or cultural immersion in the center of the city. Grenoble genuinely has something to offer for every season and kind of tourist with its breathtaking natural scenery and vibrant metropolitan culture.

Culture and Cuisine

Culture: A Melting Pot of Tradition and Innovation

Grenoble's rich history and international vibe are reflected in its broad and lively cultural scene, which is as dynamic as the city's physical environment. Grenoble welcomes a wide range of cultural influences, from antiquated customs to modern manifestations, weaving a colorful tapestry of arts, music, festivals, and more.

Historical Heritage: The city of Grenoble is replete with evidence of Roman, medieval, and Renaissance influences, all of which have left their mark on its rich cultural legacy. Magnificent architectural structures like the Notre Dame Cathedral, the Dauphiné Parliament, and the Old Town's winding cobblestone alleyways take tourists on a historical journey through time.

Galleries and Museums: The city is full of galleries and museums that display anything from modern art installations to ancient treasures. The Musée Dauphinois provides insights into the region's cultural legacy, while the Museum of Grenoble is well-known for its magnificent collection of European paintings and sculptures. Enthusiasts of modern art will value locations like the Centre d'Art Bastille and the Magasin des Horizons, which provide innovative shows and events.

Performing Arts: Grenoble is home to a flourishing performing arts scene, with a wide variety of shows held year-round in theaters, music halls, and performance venues. A range of live events, including rock concerts and classical concerts, are presented at the Summum Arena and Théâtre Municipal. The MC2: Maison de la Culture de Grenoble serves as a cultural center for theater, dance, and music.

Festivals & Events: Grenoble comes alive with a calendar of festivals and events honoring everything from food and wine to music and movies throughout the year. Rencontres Cinématographiques de Grenoble, the Cabaret Frappé, and the Grenoble Jazz Festival are just a few of the city's many exciting cultural events that draw visitors and artists from all over the world.

Cuisine: A Gastronomic Journey Through Alpine Flavors

Grenoble's cuisine, which emphasizes seasonal, fresh ingredients and substantial mountain meals, reflects its Alpine roots. Grenoble's cuisine is a feast for the senses that is likely to please food fans of all tastes, ranging from traditional recipes passed down through generations to cutting-edge culinary inventions.

Alpine Specialties: Grenoble is well-known for its meals made with seasonal ingredients including potatoes, cheese, and game meats. A popular classic is gratin dauphinois, a creamy potato gratin, while a cozy winter favorite is raclette, which is melted cheese eaten with potatoes and charcuterie. Try delicacies like fondue savoyarde, (sausages) with polenta, and tartiflette (a potato and cheese gratin) for a sense of the region's gastronomic heritage.

Market Freshness: Fresh fruit, artisanal cheeses, cured meats, and other delectable foods may be found in plenty in the city's markets. Offering the opportunity to experience the finest of Grenoble's regional cuisines and delicacies, the Marchés

Sainte-Claire and de l'Estacade are well-liked by both locals and tourists.

Innovative Dining: Grenoble is known for its traditional Alpine cuisine, but it also has a thriving culinary culture that values originality and creativity. Stylish cafés, upscale bistros, and fine dining establishments provide creative takes on traditional fare, frequently with a contemporary flair. Grenoble has cuisine to suit every taste, whether you're in the mood for basic, rustic fare or cutting-edge culinary inventions.

Wine & Spirits: A visit to Grenoble would not be complete without trying some of the local wines and spirits. Renowned for its vineyards, the Rhône Valley adjacent produces a broad range of reds, whites, and rosés that go well with regional food. Another local specialty worth trying is chartreuse, a herbal liqueur made by monks in the neighboring Chartreuse Mountains; it has a long history and diverse tastes.

Grenoble's food and culture are as lively and varied as the city itself, providing guests with a wide range of experiences to discover and savor. Grenoble delivers an unforgettable journey of discovery, whether you're indulging in the city's gastronomic pleasures or immersing yourself in its rich cultural legacy.

Exploring the City

Old Town: A Stroll Through History

Old Town: Timeless Charm Amidst Historic Splendor

The Old Town of Grenoble, sometimes referred to as the Vieille Ville, is a charming district rich in charm and history. With its meandering cobblestone lanes, medieval houses, and secret courtyards just waiting to be found, this well-preserved area, which is tucked away at the base of the Bastille hill and flanked by the Isère River, transports tourists to a bygone era.

Exploring the Cobblestone Streets

Walking around Grenoble's Old Town is like visiting a living museum, with fresh stories from the city's past being revealed around every turn. Start your trip in the Place Saint-André, a busy square with the majestic Saint-André Church in the center. Take in the ambiance of this ancient meeting area while admiring the graceful façade of the nearby buildings, many of which are from the 15th and 16th centuries. Stroll down the little Rue Saint-Laurent, which is dotted with charming stores, handmade boutiques, and welcoming cafés, starting at the Place Saint-André. Take a moment to examine the centuries-old buildings' exquisitely carved entrances and wrought-iron balconies, which individually speak to Grenoble's rich architectural history.

Look for surprising treasures hiding away behind old stone walls, secret courtyards, and hidden tunnels as you walk through the Old Town's winding alleyways. These undiscovered treasures provide a peek into Grenoble's medieval history and offer peaceful moments in the middle of the busy metropolis.

Historical Landmarks and Hidden Gems

A trip to Grenoble's Old Town wouldn't be complete without taking in some of its cultural attractions and historical sites. Head to the Place Grenette, the Grenoble Museum of Art and Archaeology location, a bustling square surrounded by old buildings. Enter to view a wide range of objects, paintings, and sculptures that chronicle Grenoble's creative history from antiquity to the present.

The nearby Maison de Saint-Hugues, with its serene courtyard and well-preserved medieval building, gives a window into Grenoble's ecclesiastical past and offers a pleasant escape from the bustle of the city.

Enjoy a stroll or a picturesque trip on the Grenoble Bastille cable car to the Fort de la Bastille for a panoramic view of the city and the surrounding Alps. This old castle, perched on a hill above Grenoble's Old Town, provides stunning views as well as an intriguing peek into the city's military history.

Culinary Delights and Cozy Cafes

Visit one of the quaint cafés or restaurants in the Old Town to indulge in a taste of Grenoble's gastronomic offerings after a day of exploring. Savor regional dishes like raclette, dauphinoise, and diots with polenta and pair them with a bottle of local wine or a cool Chartreuse liqueur.

Alternatively, head to the Marché Sainte-Claire or the Marché de l'Estacade to pick up fresh vegetables, artisanal cheeses, and other gourmet treats, then have a picnic in one of the charming squares or riverfront parks in Old Town.

Stay a bit later to experience the enchantment of Grenoble's old area as the sun sets over the magnificent Old Town rooftops. Explore its medieval lanes, take in its architectural treasures, or just take in the timeless beauty of the Old Town Grenoble's rich past awaits you on an amazing trip through time.

Bastille: Iconic Landmark Overlooking the City

Bastille: A Majestic Sentinel Watching Over Grenoble

The Bastille stronghold, which is perched high above Grenoble, is a timeless representation of fortitude, resiliency, and history. This famous site, which is perched on the Bastille hill and offers stunning views of the Isère River and the surrounding area to tourists from near and far, has long been a vital component of Grenoble's character.

A Fortress Through the Ages

The construction of the fortifications to protect Grenoble from outside threats began in the 16th century, which is when the Bastille's history began. The stronghold served as a military stronghold, a jail, and a tactical vantage point with a commanding view of the surrounding area, all of which were vital roles it played in protecting the city over the ages.

The Bastille became a global emblem of public revolt and fight against oppression during the French Revolution. After revolutionary troops took control of the stronghold in 1789, the revolution underwent a sea change, and the fortress's reputation as a symbol of liberty and independence was cemented.

Panoramic Views and Scenic Wonders

The Bastille now provides tourists with amazing views of the city below as well as a window into Grenoble's colorful history. The stronghold, which is reachable by foot, cable car, or hiking paths, invites intrepid travelers of all ages to explore its dungeons, tunnels, and walls as well as to take in the breathtaking views that go on forever.

Visitors are rewarded with a 360-degree view of Grenoble and the surrounding Alps from the summit of the Bastille. The scene is one of breathtaking natural beauty, with snow-capped peaks, lush valleys, and meandering rivers creating an image that enthralls the senses. The view from the Bastille never fails to evoke amazement and surprise, whether it is lit up by the sparkling lights of sunset or the golden light of daybreak.

Cultural Treasures and Outdoor Adventures

The Bastille is home to a multitude of cultural attractions and outdoor activities in addition to its breathtaking scenery. Discover the intricate passageways and secret rooms of the castle, where multimedia displays and interactive exhibitions vividly bring Grenoble's past to life.

The Bastille is a starting point for outdoor enthusiasts seeking adventure, as the hills and forests around it are dotted with hiking trails, rock climbing routes, and mountain biking courses. For any level of outdoor enthusiast, there is something to enjoy, from strolls to heart-pounding climbs.

Dining with a View

Relax and unwind in one of the little cafés or restaurants along the Bastille after a day of exploring. Here, you may enjoy regional delicacies and cool drinks while taking in the breathtaking surroundings. Eating at the Bastille is a memorable experience, whether you're having a fast snack or a leisurely dinner.

A Timeless Symbol of Grenoble

Grenoble's history, tenacity, and scenic beauty are embodied in the Bastille stronghold, an everlasting icon. Discovering its historic walls, taking in the expansive vistas, or going on outdoor excursions in the nearby hills, the Bastille provides an amazing trip through Grenoble's history and present that will undoubtedly leave a lasting impact on everyone who visits.

Museums and Galleries

Windows into Grenoble's Cultural Tapestry

In Grenoble's museums and galleries, visitors may fully immerse themselves in the city's rich legacy, artistic traditions, and inventive spirit, all of which are on full show due to its dynamic cultural landscape. These organizations provide a wide range of activities that reflect Grenoble's cultural fabric and encourage inquiry, creativity, and discovery, showcasing anything from antiquated antiquities to modern masterpieces.

Museum of Grenoble: A Treasure Trove of Art and History

The city's unwavering appreciation for art and culture is attested to by the Museum of Grenoble. With a collection spanning ages and countries, it is among the most important and oldest museums in France, having been founded in 1798. Visitors may take a trip through time and space as they explore the museum's halls, which feature everything from contemporary masterpieces to treasures from ancient Egypt.

The museum's collection features sculptures, pottery, and decorative arts from all over the world in addition to pieces by well-known painters including Picasso, Matisse, and Monet. The Museum of Grenoble is a must-visit location for both art lovers and history fans because of its interactive displays and multimedia projects, which offer context and insight into the pieces on show.

Musée Dauphinois: Exploring Regional Heritage

To gain a more profound comprehension of Grenoble's cultural legacy, one need just visit the Musée Dauphinois. The history, customs, and way of life of the Dauphiné area are the focus of this museum, which is housed in a former convent with a view of the city. Visitors may explore subjects ranging from industry and immigration to rural life and folklore via immersive exhibitions, multimedia presentations, and hands-on activities, gaining insights into the people and places that have influenced Grenoble's character over the ages.

In addition, the Musée Dauphinois presents seminars, cultural events, and temporary exhibitions that honor the richness and inventiveness of the area. This vibrant cultural institution offers a plethora of fascinating new experiences, from folk festivals to modern art exhibits.

Contemporary Art Spaces: Pushing Boundaries and Inspiring Innovation

Grenoble is home to a strong contemporary art scene, with galleries and exhibition venues that feature cutting-edge works by local and international artists, in addition to its conventional institutions. Located next to the Isère River in a former warehouse, the Magasin des Horizons is a preeminent hub for modern art and culture, offering talks, performances, and exhibitions that subvert stereotypes and provoke thought.

Visit the Centre d'Art Bastille, housed in a 19th-century fort with views of Old Town, for avant-garde art in a historic setting. This distinctive cultural venue invites people to interact with art in novel and surprising ways through its exhibits, artist residencies, and experimental initiatives that examine the nexus between art, technology, and society.

Cultural Exploration and Discovery

Grenoble's museums and galleries provide a multitude of chances for cultural study and discovery, regardless of your level of expertise or if you're just a curious visitor looking for inspiration. These organizations provide visitors an opportunity to explore Grenoble's history, present, and future through a variety of items, from antiquated objects to modern works of art, offering a glimpse into the city's vibrant cultural scene and rich legacy. Come explore and discover for yourself the richness and beauty of Grenoble's cultural tapestry.

Culinary Delights: Where to Eat and Drink

Indulge in Grenoble's Gastronomic Wonders

The culinary scene in Grenoble is a sensory extravaganza, offering a mouthwatering variety of flavors, ingredients, and dining experiences all waiting to be discovered. Food lovers of all tastes will be delighted by the city's restaurants, cafés, and markets, which provide a gastronomic adventure ranging from inventive fusion cuisine to classic Alpine delicacies.

Bistros and Brasseries: Savoring Tradition

Visit one of the numerous bistros and brasseries in the city for a taste of traditional Grenoble cuisine in a welcoming atmosphere, where substantial meals and friendly service are the main attractions. Situated in the center of the Old Town, Le Bouchon des Filles offers classic French cuisine with a contemporary touch. It highlights Grenoble's culinary legacy with its inventive presentations and use of fresh ingredients.

Another well-liked cafe, La Ferme à Dédé, is renowned for its farm-to-table cuisine and rustic atmosphere. This family-run restaurant specializes in regional favorites like tartiflette, raclette, and idiots with polenta, all produced with locally sourced ingredients and served with a side of friendly friendliness. It is located in a lovely courtyard a short distance from the Place Grenette.

Gourmet Dining: Haute Cuisine in the Alps

Book a seat at one of Grenoble's gourmet restaurants for a sophisticated eating experience that highlights the creativity and craftsmanship of the region's culinary industry. Located in the posh Europole neighborhood, L'Épicurien serves elegant cuisine with a focus on French and Mediterranean cuisines. The meals are visually stunning and have mouthwatering flavors.

Housed in a historic home with a view of the Place Victor Hugo, Le Fantin Latour is another fine dining establishment that is well-known for its inventive food and flawless service. Under the direction of Michelin-starred chef Stéphane Froidevaux, the eatery serves up innovative cuisine that will satisfy even the pickiest palates by showcasing fresh ingredients.

Cafes and Bakeries: A Taste of Everyday Life

Spend some time touring Grenoble's bakeries and cafes, where inhabitants congregate to enjoy pastries, coffee, and conversation, to get a glimpse of daily life there. In the heart of the Place aux Herbes, Café de la Table Ronde is a well-liked location for people-watching and enjoying a leisurely breakfast or lunch.

Visit Pâtisserie Chocolaterie Weiss, a neighborhood landmark renowned for its mouth watering pastries, chocolates, and confections, for a sweet treat. Every taste, from delicate macarons to rich chocolate truffles, is a tribute to the skill and artistry of Grenoble's pastry chefs.

Market Fare: Fresh and Flavorful

A trip to one of Grenoble's lively markets, where merchants sell artisanal cheeses, cured meats, fresh fruit, and other gourmet treats, would complete any stay. Situated in the center of the Old Town, the Marché Sainte-Claire is a well-liked attraction for both residents and tourists, providing a colorful selection of seasonal foodstuffs and specialized goods.

Explore the Marché de l'Estacade, where international merchants congregate to offer spices, herbs, teas, and other exotic items, to get a sense of Grenoble's culinary variety. Grenoble's markets will tantalize your senses and pique your stomach, whether you're preparing for a picnic or are just perusing for ideas.

Raise a Glass: Toasting to Grenoble's Spirits

Try some of the regional wines, beers, and spirits from Grenoble to go with your gastronomic explorations. Prominent for its vineyards, the Rhône Valley is close by and produces an extensive range of reds, whites, and rosés that go well with the city's delectable food.

Seek Chartreuse, a herbal liqueur made by monks in the neighboring Chartreuse Mountains, for a flavor of Grenoble's distinctive history. Toast to the centuries-old legacy of craftsmanship and conviviality in Grenoble by sipping it neat or mixing it into a traditional cocktail.

Bon Appétit: A Culinary Adventure Awaits

There are many delicious options available in Grenoble's culinary scene that are just waiting to be sampled. Every meal is an opportunity to sample the rich flavors and friendly friendliness of this energetic city, whether you're treating yourself to a cup of coffee and a croissant at a sidewalk café or indulging in traditional Alpine food. Come explore and experience a gastronomic journey that will leave you wanting more. Salutations!

Outdoor Adventures

Hiking in the French Alps

Exploring Nature's Playground

The French Alps are a hiker's dream come true because of its untamed lakes, lush valleys, and craggy peaks, which create a breathtaking setting for outdoor exploration. Experience the beauty and peacefulness of the Alpine terrain on paths and routes tailored to suit all skill levels and fitness levels, whether you're an experienced climber or just a casual nature lover.

Choosing Your Adventure

Selecting the appropriate path for your ability level and interests is one of the first things you should do when organizing a hiking vacation in the French Alps. With hiking experiences ranging from easy strolls through meadows to strenuous climbs of towering peaks, the Alps have something for every type of hiker.

Many simple to moderate paths meander through picturesque valleys, meadows, and woodlands, providing stunning vistas without requiring technical abilities or specific equipment, making them ideal for families and novices. The Vanoise National Park, Écrins National Park, and Chamonix Valley are popular locations for leisurely treks. There, well-marked paths and quaint mountain chalets offer a convenient and accessible hiking experience.

For more accomplished hikers looking for a challenge, there are plenty of high-altitude hiking and mountaineering alternatives in the French Alps. Reaching the top of famous mountains like Mont Blanc, the Matterhorn, and the Aiguille du Midi takes technical know-how, appropriate

gear, and meticulous preparation, but the rewards are unmatched vistas and a lifelong sense of accomplishment.

Preparing for Your Hike

It's crucial to make sure you're outfitted and ready for any mountainous circumstances before starting your hiking trip. The following are some vital pointers to remember:

Check the weather forecast: The weather in the Alps is subject to sudden fluctuations, so make sure you check the forecast before you go and pack accordingly for variations in temperature, precipitation, and visibility.

Dress in layers: Layer up to be warm and dry in the unpredictable weather. Don't forget to bring a waterproof jacket and pants in case of rain or snow.

Pack essential gear: Bring a first aid kit, water, food, a map, a compass, or a GPS device, along with any other necessary equipment you might need for your trek. In case of emergency, it's also a good idea to carry a satellite communicator or cell phone.

Respect the environment: Keep to authorized routes, pack away your waste, and show consideration for the local wildlife and flora. Assist in conserving the Alps' splendor for the enjoyment of future generations.

Enjoying the Experience

Spend some time enjoying the route and taking in the splendor of your surroundings once you're out on it. Make regular stops to refuel, take in the scenery, and rest. Also, don't forget to snap lots of pictures to preserve the memories of your journey.

Numerous natural treasures may be seen along the route, including towering cliffs, glaciers, and brilliant wildflowers in addition to tumbling waterfalls. Listen for the peaceful sounds of mountain streams and bird music, and keep a lookout for animals like ibex, chamois, and marmots.

Hiking in the French Alps is a once-in-a-lifetime opportunity to push yourself, connect with nature, and make lifelong memories. The Alps provide a world of adventure just waiting to be discovered, whether you want to scale majestic peaks or wander through serene valleys. So grab your backpack and lace your boots, and let's go out into the French Alps, nature's playground.

Skiing and Snowboarding

Skiing and Snowboarding in the French Alps: Embrace Winter's Playground

The French Alps are well-known across the world for offering amazing skiing and snowboarding experiences, drawing visitors from all over the world who like winter sports. For skiers and snowboarders of all skill levels, from novices to specialists, the Alps provide an unmatched playground with its expansive ski resorts, smooth slopes, and stunning mountain scenery. The French Alps offer something for everyone, whether you're looking for heart-pounding descents, routes suitable for families, or charming mountain towns.

Choosing Your Resort

When organizing a trip to the French Alps for skiing or snowboarding, one of the first things to do is pick the best resort for your tastes and degree of experience. Here are a few well-liked choices to think about:

Chamonix: dubbed the "Gateway to the Alps," Chamonix has some of Europe's most difficult terrain, including the well-known Vallée Blanche off-piste run. Experienced skiers and thrill seekers love Chamonix for its vibrant apres-ski culture and breathtaking vistas of Mont Blanc.

Courchevel: A component of the vast Three Valleys ski region, Courchevel is well-known for its opulent resorts, first-rate facilities, and an abundance of terrain suitable for all skill levels of skiers and snowboarders. Courchevel provides a traditional French skiing experience with its well-maintained slopes, quaint mountain villages, and fine eating establishments.

Val d'Isère and Tignes: Part of the Espace Killy ski region, these mountains provide dependable snow conditions, high-altitude skiing, and an exciting après-ski culture. This region is a favorite among families and groups of friends because it offers a variety of terrain, from moderate beginning slopes to steep couloirs and powder-filled bowls.

Les Deux Alpes: A favored spot for summertime skiing and freestyle fans, Les Deux Alpes boasts a lively environment and vast glacier skiing. In addition to a thriving town center with stores, dining options, and vibrant nightlife, the resort features a snowpark, a halfpipe, and plenty of off-piste opportunities.

Megève: Known for its picturesque skiing terrain, ancient architecture, and quaint village ambiance, Megève is tucked away in the shadow of Mont Blanc. Megève's tree-lined lines, mild slopes, and charming landscape make it a well-liked option for families and couples looking for a romantic winter escape.

Making the Most of Your Trip

It's time to get to the slopes and maximize your French Alps skiing or snowboarding experience once you've selected your destination. The following advice can help you have a memorable experience:

Take lessons: Learning from a skilled instructor may help you explore new terrain safely, develop your technique, and boost your confidence whether you're a beginner, an expert skier, or a snowboarder.

Explore the terrain: From easy beginning slopes to strenuous black diamond lines, the French Alps offer a vast range of terrain for skiers and snowboarders of all skill levels. Spend some time exploring the resort's various locations to find new routes and powder stashes.

Stay safe: When skiing or snowboarding in the Alps, being safe should always come first. Always wear a helmet, know the resort's safety regulations, and only ski or ride to the level of your ability.

Enjoy the apres-ski: After spending the day on the mountains, unwind and have a meal or a drink at one of the resort's welcoming mountain eateries or après-ski bars. In the heart of the French Alps, experience the spirit of winter's playground by telling friends and fellow skiers about your activities.

The French Alps provide an exhilarating combination of adventure, excitement, and scenic beauty for skiing and snowboarding that is sure to enthrall and motivate. The Alps provide an incredible winter experience that will make you want to go back year after year, whether you're carving turns down high powder slopes, driving through charming mountain communities, or enjoying hot chocolate by a crackling fire. Prepare to enjoy winter's playground in the magnificent French Alps by packing your skis or snowboard, layering on your warmest clothing, and hitting the slopes.

Cycling Routes Around Grenoble

Pedal Through Alpine Beauty

Bike enthusiasts will find a cyclist's dream in Grenoble and the surrounding area, with beautiful views of the French Alps, strenuous climbs, and thrilling descents. Every type of rider will find something to enjoy in and around Grenoble, whether they are road bikers looking for challenging passes, mountain bikers seeking rough routes, or leisure riders seeking beautiful scenery.

Road Cycling: Conquer the Mountain Passes

The French Alps are a great location for road cyclists, with picturesque mountain passes, twisting roads, and expansive vistas around every corner. Grenoble is a great starting point for touring some of the most famous bicycle routes in the area, such as:

Col de la Croix de Fer: Because of its breathtaking landscape and strong slopes, riders love this strenuous climb. Riding the Col de la Croix de Fer may be done as part of a circle that starts in Grenoble and includes other well-known climbs like the Col du Glandon and the Col du Galibier.

Alpe d'Huez: Renowned for its 21 hairpin bends and strenuous incline, Alpe d'Huez is an absolute must-ride for riders looking to put their climbing skills to the test. Riders may climb the mountain and take in breath-taking vistas of the surrounding peaks by beginning at the town of Bourg d'Oisans.

Col du Lautaret and Col du Galibier: This loop provides breathtaking views of glaciers, snow-capped summits, and alpine meadows, making it a must-do activity for anyone seeking a traditional Alpine experience. A swift descent down to Grenoble completes the thrilling yet difficult ascent to the top of the Galibier.

Mountain Biking: Thrills in the Wild

The Grenoble region has a vast network of trails and courses that suit riders of all skill levels, providing mountain bikers with an abundance of excitement and adventure. There is a path for you to explore, including difficult singletrack, flowing descents, and spectacular alpine excursions.

Les 2 Alpes Bike Park: Offering some of the greatest mountain riding in the French Alps, Les 2 Alpes Bike Park has over 90 kilometers of tracks and a vertical drop of 2,600 meters. There is riding for cyclists of all ability levels, from easy green trails for beginners to challenging black diamond runs.

Chartreuse Mountains: The Chartreuse Mountains provide a range of mountain biking options, including cross-country routes, difficult descents, and thrilling backcountry excursions. The mountains are only a short drive from Grenoble. The paths that round Saint-Pierre-de-Chartreuse are especially well-liked because they offer breathtaking views of the hills and valleys in the area.

Vercors Regional Natural Park: With a network of routes winding through rocky limestone cliffs, lush woods, and alpine meadows, the Vercors Regional Natural Park is a mountain biker's dream come true. The trails surrounding the town of Villard-de-Lans, the Grand Veymont loop, and the Pas des Bachassons descent are among the highlights.

Leisure Cycling: Scenic Rides for Everyone

Grenoble and its environs provide a range of leisurely rides and picturesque routes that highlight the region's natural beauty without requiring strenuous climbs or tricky terrain for cyclists looking for a slower pace. Several well-liked choices consist of:

Isère River Bike Path: This level cycle route offers breathtaking views of the surrounding mountains and countryside as it follows the Isère River from Grenoble to the charming town of Romans-sur-Isère.

Lakeside Loop: Take a leisurely circular ride that passes by Lac de Monteynard-Avignonet, Lac de Laffrey, and Lac de Paladru, among other serene lakes and quaint villages in the Grenoble region. There are lots of possibilities for swimming, picnicking, and sightseeing along the route.

Vineyard Tour: Explore the Rhône Valley's vineyards and wineries by bicycle along this lovely route that passes through charming villages, rolling hills, and sun-drenched vineyards. You'll get the chance to taste regional wines and delectable foods as you go.

A world of excitement awaits cyclists in and around Grenoble, with breathtaking mountain passes, rough trails, and picturesque routes suitable for riders of all skill levels and interests. Everyone may enjoy cycling in Grenoble and the surrounding area, regardless of their preference for road cycling, mountain biking, or leisurely riding through picturesque areas with breathtaking descents or views. So prepare to cycle across the breathtakingly beautiful French Alps after grabbing your bike and donning your helmet.

Paragliding and Other Airborne Activities

Paragliding and Other Airborne Adventures: Soar Above the French Alps

Grenoble and the surrounding area provide a plethora of exhilarating aerial sports for thrill-seekers and adventure seekers, ranging from skydiving and hot-air ballooning to hang gliding and paragliding. The French Alps offer the ideal setting for amazing aerial experiences that will leave you speechless and ecstatic because of its breathtaking mountain landscape, ideal weather, and knowledgeable instructors.

Paragliding: Soar Like a Bird

One of the most well-liked aerial pursuits in the Grenoble region is paragliding, which provides a singular chance to glide through the sky like a bird and enjoy breathtaking vistas of the surrounding lakes, valleys, and mountains. There are alternatives for every degree of skill, whether you're a seasoned paragliding pro or a beginner, like:

Tandem Flights: Take a tandem paragliding flight with a qualified instructor to feel the rush of the sport. You'll be flying high over the Alps in no time at all if you strap into a harness, sprint a few steps, and experience the weightlessness that comes with gliding through the air.

Instructional Courses: There are instructional courses that cover everything from fundamental flight skills to advanced maneuvers for people who want to master the art of paragliding. Skilled educators offer practical instruction and direction, enabling you to acquire the abilities and self-assurance required to soar alone.

Cross-Country Flying: After you've learned the fundamentals, you can go on thrilling cross-country flights over the Alps, experiencing everything from thermalling high above the mountains to soaring ridge lines. Pilots with experience who want to test their boundaries and explore new territory can sign up for guided tours and adventures.

Hang Gliding: Experience True Freedom

Hang gliding is an exhilarating way to feel like you're flying while taking in breathtaking views of the Alpine scenery for those looking for a more traditional aerial experience. Using the strength of the wind to remain aloft and maneuver precisely, a hang glider's elegant shape and lightweight construction let you glide through the air with ease.

Tandem hang gliding: Like tandem paragliding, tandem hang gliding lets you enjoy the rush of flight while being supervised by a qualified instructor. A surge of excitement will fill you as you strap into a tandem harness, launch from a picturesque mountain crest, and soar through the skies while taking in expansive vistas of the Alps below.

Solo Flying: For seasoned pilots, solo hang gliding provides the utmost liberty and self-sufficiency to experience the sky at your own pace. You can launch from approved locations throughout the area and go on solitary flights that take you to new heights and views if you have the necessary training and certification.

Skydiving: Dive into the Blue

Skydiving provides an unmatched sensation of freefalling from thousands of feet above the ground and softly parachuting down to land for the ultimate adrenaline thrill. Grenoble provides a variety of skydiving experiences, suitable for both novice and expert jumpers. These possibilities include:

Tandem Skydives: Leap into the exhilaration of skydiving under the supervision of a qualified instructor. Following a quick training session, you'll board an aircraft, take off, reach altitude, and then jump out of it. You'll fall at a maximum speed of 120 mph before using your parachute to enjoy a breathtaking canopy ride down to Earth.

Solo Skydives: Grenoble provides options for solitary jumps at certain drop zones across the region for experienced skydivers. Skydiving in the French Alps is an amazing experience that will leave you wanting more, whether you're practicing formation flying, perfecting your canopy control, or just enjoying the feeling of freefall.

Hot Air Ballooning: Drift on the Breeze

Hot air ballooning is a relaxing method to enjoy the grandeur of the Alpine scenery from above, providing a more tranquil aerial experience. Take in expansive vistas of snow-capped peaks, verdant valleys, and quaint villages below as you glide easily through the sky, guided by the wind and framed by the mountains.

Scenic Flights: During one to two hours, hot air balloon tours in the Grenoble region take you on a picturesque adventure through the heart of the Alps. Experienced pilots will provide commentary and point out places of interest as you soar above the countryside, allowing you to witness the dawn or sunset from the comfort of the basket.

Special Events: Hot air balloon festivals and activities that highlight the elegance and spectacle of ballooning are held in Grenoble all year long. A rare chance to witness the wonders of hot air ballooning in the French Alps, these events feature everything from competitive races and aerial shows to mass ascensions and night glows.

Grenoble and the surrounding area offer a world of aerial activities just waiting to be discovered, whether you're floating softly in a hot air balloon or zooming through the sky on a hang glider, paraglider, or skydiving. The breathtaking mountain landscape, ideal weather, and knowledgeable instructors make the French Alps the ideal setting for life-changing aerial adventures that will inspire and exhilarate you. So gather your courage, get ready for takeoff, and get ready to fly above the Alps' amazing grandeur.

Day Trips and Excursions

Chartreuse Mountains: A Day in Nature

Chartreuse Mountains: A Day in Nature's Embrace

Take in the peace and beauty of the Chartreuse Mountains, a pristine natural wonderland only a short drive from Grenoble, as an escape from the rush of city life. The Chartreuse region provides countless chances for outdoor exploration, leisure, and renewal with its verdant woods, lofty peaks, and glistening lakes. The Chartreuse Mountains provide activities to suit all types of hikers, from strenuous treks to strolls to quiet getaways in the great outdoors.

Morning: Rise and Shine in the Mountains

Head to one of the numerous little towns, like Saint-Pierre-de-Chartreuse or Saint-Pierre-d'Entremont, tucked away in the heart of the Chartreuse Mountains, early in the morning. Savor a substantial breakfast at a neighborhood bakery or cafe to prepare yourself for the activities that lie ahead.

Put on your hiking boots and head out for a morning trek through the beautiful Chartreuse Mountains wilderness after breakfast. There are routes to suit every experience and fitness level, whether you're an experienced hiker searching for a strenuous ascent or a casual nature lover looking for a stroll.

Midday: Picnic in Paradise

Take some time to stop and enjoy the stunning beauty of your surroundings while you hike. Choose a lovely location to pause for a picnic lunch; it might be next to a serene mountain stream or with a view of an exquisite alpine meadow. Stow away some fresh bread, seasonal fruits, cured meats, and cheeses from the area, and have a leisurely dinner while taking in the sights and sounds of nature.

After lunch, go on with your trek or explore the region more, looking for local animals like marmots, chamois, and ibex that inhabit the Chartreuse Mountains. Take in the breathtaking views, inhale the clean mountain air, and let your cares fade away as you lose yourself in the splendor of the natural world.

Afternoon: Explore Hidden Gems

Explore some of the Chartreuse Mountains' hidden treasures by going off the main track in the afternoon. Discover the intriguing history and customs of the Carthusian monks who have lived in the area for centuries by visiting one of the old monasteries in the area, such as the Grande Chartreuse or the Monastery of the Reposoir.

Alternatively, visit one of the quaint towns in the vicinity, such as Saint-Pierre-de-Chartreuse or Saint-Pierre-d'Entremont, where you can meander around the little cobblestone alleys, peruse the wares of local artisans, and savor regional delicacies like blueberry tart or Chartreuse liqueur.

Evening: Relax and Unwind

Choose a serene area to relax as the day comes to an end and observe the sun setting over the mountains, illuminating the surrounding area with a golden hue. Enjoy the sense of calm and quiet that comes from spending time in nature's embrace while you think back on the experiences of the day.

Return to Grenoble or one of the neighboring towns in the evening, and spoil yourself with a delectable dinner at a neighborhood eatery. Here, you may experience the local specialties and raise a glass to a memorable day spent in the Chartreuse Mountains. The cuisine and warmth of the area are guaranteed to make an impact, whether you're enjoying gourmet treats or hearty mountain fare.

A day spent in the Chartreuse Mountains provides an opportunity to re-establish a connection with nature and a much-needed reprieve from the demands of contemporary life. Enjoying a picnic in the fresh mountain air, trekking through unspoiled nature, or simply taking in the beauty and calm of the Chartreuse region will leave you feeling rejuvenated, invigorated, and inspired. So gather your spirit of adventure and head to the stunning Chartreuse Mountains for a day spent in the embrace of nature.

Vercors Regional Natural Park

Vercors Regional Natural Park: Discover Nature's Hidden Gem
The Vercors Regional Natural Park is a refuge of natural beauty, rich biodiversity, and outdoor adventure waiting to be discovered. It is tucked away in the heart of the French Alps. With its diverse terrain that includes alpine meadows, thick woods, and craggy limestone cliffs, the park provides countless chances for mountain biking, hiking, and animal viewing. The Vercors has something for everyone to appreciate, whether you're looking for heart-pounding thrills or serene moments.

Explore the Great Outdoors
With a network of hiking paths winding through a variety of habitats and landscapes, the Vercors Regional Natural Park is a hiker's dream, catering to all skill levels. There are trails for every taste and

skill level, from easy walks along winding rivers to strenuous climbs of high summits.

Take a stroll along one of the numerous designated routes that wind through the park, including the Cirque d'Archiane or the Balcony of the Vercors, for a leisurely introduction. In addition to providing expansive views of the nearby mountains and valleys, these picturesque trails provide chances to see animals like chamois, ibex, and golden eagles.

Discover Hidden Treasures

Look for the park's hidden gems as you explore the Vercors, such as enigmatic caverns, gushing waterfalls, and historic ruins that provide insights into the area's complex geological and historical past. See breathtaking subterranean formations at the Grotte de Choranche or the Grottes de la Balme, or go to the Cascade de la Pissoire or the Cascade de la Draye Blanche to take in the grandeur and majesty of tumbling waterfalls.

Visit the medieval town of Saint-Antoine-l'Abbaye or the historic village of Pont-en-Royans for a glimpse into the history of the area. Here, you can discover the customs and way of life of the people who have lived in the Vercors for centuries, explore quaint cobblestone streets, and take in the stunning architecture.

Experience Alpine Adventure

The Vercors offer a multitude of chances for adventure and excitement for those who are addicted to adrenaline and seek thrills. Try your mettle on one of the area's top-notch rock climbing routes, take on strenuous mountain biking courses, or attempt paragliding or hang gliding for an aerial perspective of the breathtaking scenery below.

The Vercors becomes a winter paradise in the winter, offering chances for cross-country skiing, snowboarding, snowshoeing, and skiing among snow-covered peaks and pure woods. The Vercors provide something for any winter sports enthusiast to enjoy, whether they like serene Nordic routes or steep descents.

Preserving Natural Beauty

Be mindful of the fragile balance of nature and walk softly when exploring the Vercors Regional Natural Park. Keep to designated routes, remove any litter, and observe the Leave No Trace, Use the "Trace" principles to reduce your environmental effects and contribute to maintaining the park's natural beauty for the enjoyment of future generations.

In the center of the French Alps, the Vercors Regional Natural Park is a hidden treasure just waiting to be found. It offers a special fusion of outdoor activity, natural beauty, and cultural legacy. The Vercors provide activities for all types of visitors, including trekking through pristine nature, discovering secret caverns, and skiing down snow-covered slopes. So gather your courage and head out to discover this magnificent natural haven.

Annecy: The Venice of the Alps

Annecy: Exploring the Venice of the Alps

The charming town of Annecy is located at the northernmost point of Lake Annecy and is encircled by gorgeous scenery and snow-capped mountains. Known as the

"Venice of the Alps" because of its picturesque old town, network of canals, and cobblestone streets, Annecy is a location that enthralls tourists with its romantic atmosphere, extensive history, and breathtaking natural beauty. A plethora of activities await you in Annecy, whether you choose to explore ancient sites, indulge in regional cuisine, or take a stroll along the shoreline.

A Walk Along the Quays

Take a stroll along the Thiou River's quays to start your tour of Annecy, as it meanders through the center of the town. Take in the vibrant architecture, charming bridges bordered with flowers, and lively cafés that adorn the banks of the quiet canals. Don't forget to see the elegant swans that swim by.

The Pont des Amours (Bridge of Love), a charming footbridge with expansive views of the river and surrounding mountains, is a must-see location. Lovebirds and romantics alike frequent the bridge because of the legend that those who kiss there will experience eternal love and bliss.

Exploring the Old Town

Enter Annecy's medieval old town, a charming labyrinth of small alleys and lanes, from the quays. Admire the exquisitely maintained medieval building, with flower-filled balconies, pastel-colored walls, and elaborately carved wooden shutters.

Explore the cobblestone alleys to find secret tunnels that take you back in time, quaint squares, and secret courtyards. Make sure to explore the Palais de l'Isle, a former jail and medieval castle situated on a tiny island in the Thiou River, to discover more about the intriguing past of the town and its people.

A Taste of Savoyard Cuisine

A trip to Annecy wouldn't be complete without indulging in some of the mouthwatering Savoy food. Savor robust meals like fondue, raclette, and tartiflette, which are cooked with regional cheeses, potatoes, and charcuterie, and are served with a crisp white wine from the surrounding vineyards.

Savor a slice of tarte aux myrtilles, a regional delicacy prepared with a sweet pastry crust and fresh blueberries harvested from the nearby mountains, for dessert. For a taste of true Savoyard hospitality, wash it down with a shot of génépi, a traditional herbal liqueur created from Alpine plants.

Outdoor Adventures

With its breathtaking natural surroundings, Annecy provides a plethora of adventure activities for outdoor lovers. Take a bike rental and cruise the picturesque cycling routes around Lake Annecy, pausing along the way for a dip, a picnic, or just lounging in the sun.

Alternatively, get out on the water and hire a rowboat, paddleboard, or kayak to explore the lake's glistening waters at your speed. As you glide across the river, take in the breathtaking vistas of the surrounding mountains and woods. Keep a look out for local animals, including beavers, swans, and herons.

With its enchanting canals, ancient buildings, and breathtaking natural beauty, Annecy genuinely lives up to its moniker as the Venice of the Alps, captivating tourists from near and far. Discover the many pleasures that Annecy has to offer, whether you're eating local cuisine, wandering along the waterfront, or touring the ancient town. So gather your belongings, embark on a tour of this charming town, and be ready to fall head over heels with the Venice of the Alps.

Nightlife and Entertainment

Bars and Cafes

Bars and Cafés: Savoring Annecy's Culinary Scene

Beyond its delectable Savoyard food, Annecy has a thriving culinary scene that includes a variety of quaint restaurants and cafés where residents and tourists alike congregate to relax, mingle, and enjoy the tastes of the area. There are many different locations in Annecy to suit every taste and occasion, ranging from intimate cafés selling freshly made coffee and pastries to bustling pubs serving specialty cocktails and regional wines.

Morning Coffee and Pastries

Visit one of the little cafés in Annecy to begin your day with a leisurely breakfast of freshly made coffee and pastries while taking in the atmosphere of the quaint surroundings. For a traditional French breakfast of croissants and café au lait, visit Café des Arts or Café du Rhône. For specialty coffee and vegan pastries prepared with ingredients that are found locally, check out Café Bunna.

Don't pass up the opportunity to try some regional delicacies like tarte aux myrtilles (blueberry tart) or bugnes (fried dough pastries), which go great with hot cocoa or a steaming cup of coffee on a cool morning. These will give you a flavor of Annecy's culinary heritage.

Lunchtime Delights

When midday arrives, stroll through the busy streets of Annecy to find a selection of cafés and bistros that provide mouthwatering lunch selections to satisfy any appetite. For a classic Savoyard meal of tartiflette or raclette, stop into Le Café des Ducs. Pair it with a fresh white wine from the surrounding vineyards.

Try Le Pain Quotidien or La Bolée Savoyarde for a lighter choice. They provide a variety of freshly produced salads, quiches, and sandwiches created with ingredients that are acquired locally. For the ideal lunchtime treat, enjoy your meal with a glass of sparkling cider or craft beer from one of Annecy's small brewers.

Afternoon Tea and Treats

Take a breather and enjoy some afternoon tea and pastries at one of Annecy's quaint tea rooms or patisseries after a full morning of touring. Try Salon de Thé Le Thé des Alpes for a variety of artisanal teas and sweet sweets, or Pâtisserie Chez Pascal for a delicious assortment of pastries, cakes, and macarons.

Treat yourself to a delicious afternoon tea at Le Clos des Sens for a genuinely luxurious experience. You may relish a variety of savory sandwiches, scones, and pastries served with a pot of freshly made tea or champagne.

Evening Cocktails and Nightlife

The town of Annecy comes alive at night as the sun sets, with a selection of pubs and clubs providing excellent wines, delectable drinks, and live music to keep you engaged far into the morning. For well-made cocktails and a buzzing atmosphere, visit Le Barista or Le Comptoir de la Bourse. Alternatively, try Le Bar du Carnot for a variety of regional wines and beers served in a warm, welcoming environment.

Attend a live performance at one of the numerous pubs or music venues in Annecy for a flavor of the town's cultural life. You may hear anything from jazz and blues to rock and techno music late into the night.

There are many different places in Annecy to suit every taste and occasion, whether you're having coffee in a quaint café, treating yourself to afternoon tea and pastries, or taking in drinks and live music in a bustling bar. So gather your hunger, get out to sample the town's cuisine, and get ready to enjoy Annecy's delicacies in style.

Performing Arts and Music Scene

Performing Arts and Music Scene: Annecy's Cultural Heartbeat

The dynamic blend of live music, performing arts, and entertainment that characterizes Annecy's cultural scene makes it a must-visit location for both music fans and culture vultures. The town of Annecy provides a wide range of cultural events that are a reflection of its rich legacy and creative energy, from classic theaters and modern galleries to vibrant street performers and exciting music venues.

Theater and Performance

Experience the world of theater and performance in one of the iconic locations in Annecy. Here, you can see a range of live events, from modern plays and experimental pieces to traditional theater and dance.

See the best-performing arts venue in Annecy, the Théâtre Bonlieu, which presents a year-round schedule of multimedia, dance, music, and theater performances by regional and foreign performers. At Théâtre Bonlieu, there's always something fascinating going on, from provocative plays to cutting-edge dance works.

Visit Le Rabelais, a little theater in the center of the old town, for a more personal theatrical experience. Here, you may see anything from comedy and cabaret to puppetry and children's theater.

Live Music and Concerts

The live music scene in Annecy is thriving, with several different venues hosting concerts and live performances all year long. With Annecy's diverse music culture, you may find something to fit your preferences in jazz, blues, rock, or electronic music.

Visit Le Brise Glace, the best music venue in Annecy, for a varied program of shows and events that include both national and international performers. Music lovers of all stripes may find something to enjoy at Le Brise Glace, from known acts to up-and-coming indie bands.

Visit Le Forum, a small pub and live music venue in the center of the old town, for a more relaxed atmosphere. Le Forum is the ideal spot to unwind with a drink and take in some live music in a laid-back atmosphere thanks to its compact location and diverse array of performers.

Street Performers and Festivals

Take a stroll around the town center to get a sense of the vibrant energy of Annecy's streets. There, you may frequently see street entertainers, singers, and painters showcasing their abilities to onlookers.

Summertime in Annecy means a plethora of festivals and cultural events honoring performance, art, and music. Don't miss the

Annecy International Animated Film Festival, which features the finest in animated film from across the globe, or the Fête du Lac, a magnificent fireworks display accompanied by music and light shows that takes place on the banks of Lake Annecy every August.

The town's rich history and inventive spirit are reflected in the lively tapestry of live music, entertainment, and performing arts that make up Annecy's cultural scene. The cultural center of Annecy is always bustling with activity, whether you're taking in a concert in a historic theater, dancing the night away at a live music venue, or taking in the vibes of a street festival. So grab your sense of adventure, take in the lively arts and culture of the town, and get ready to be enthralled with Annecy's creative spirit.

Nighttime Views and Activities

Annecy's Enchanting Twilight

The town of Annecy is bathed in a mystical fantasy as the sun sets, enhanced by the shimmering reflections of Lake Annecy and the gentle glow of streetlights. There are plenty of things to do in this charming Alpine town after dark, from romantic strolls along the shoreline to exciting nightlife and cultural events.

Lakeside Strolls and Sunset Views

Start your evening with a stroll around Lake Annecy's quays, where you can take in the atmosphere of the shoreline and watch the sunset over the surrounding mountains. Walk hand in hand with your special someone down the Pont des Amours, often known as the Bridge of Love, where lovers gather to watch the sunset and exchange lucky kisses.

Rent a rowboat or pedal boat and head out on the lake as the sun sets for a romantic paddle as the colors of the sky reflect off the water's surface. This will be a once-in-a-lifetime event.

Al Fresco Dining and Gourmet Delights

Your evening stroll will have worked up an appetite. Then, reward yourself with a delectable meal at one of Annecy's many quaint cafés or restaurants, where you can enjoy the local delicacies in a lovely setting.

Enjoy fresh seafood, Savoyard delicacies, and great wines while dining al fresco on the patio of a lakeside restaurant and taking in the views and sounds of the lively waterfront.

Visit one of the charming bistros or brasseries hidden away in the old town's narrow lanes for a more private dining experience. There, you can enjoy classic French cuisine prepared with ingredients obtained locally and delivered with a side of friendly service.

Nightlife and Cocktails

Explore Annecy's exciting nightlife scene as the evening wears on. You'll discover a range of restaurants, taverns, and nightclubs that provide a fun environment and delectable cocktails to suit every taste. For well-made drinks and a sophisticated setting, visit Le Rabelais or Le Comptoir de la Bourse. For a more laid-back atmosphere with a variety of regional beers and wines, try Le Barista.

Le Brise Glace, Annecy's finest music venue, offers a range of concerts and events with both local and worldwide bands. It's a great place to see live music and entertainment. At Le Brise Glace, there's always something fascinating going on stage, with anything from jazz and blues to rock and techno music.

Cultural Events and Nighttime Festivities

Every year, Annecy comes alive with a plethora of cultural events and evening celebrations honoring art, music, and culture. Take advantage of the opportunity to see a live show in one of the town's historic theaters, or visit one of the many summertime street festivals and outdoor concerts.

With Christmas markets, holiday concerts, and seasonal activities, Annecy's streets are turned into a mystical paradise of dazzling lights and festive decorations during the winter, providing plenty of opportunity to celebrate the spirit of the season with loved ones.

There are plenty of evening activities in Annecy to fit every taste and occasion, whether you're dancing the night away at a vibrant nightclub, taking a romantic stroll along the lake, or indulging in fine dining at a waterfront restaurant. Take in the allure of this alpine village after dark, and be ready to be mesmerized by Annecy's nocturnal beauty and charm.

Practical Information

Transportation in Grenoble

Navigating the Gateway to the French Alps

Situated at the base of the French Alps, Grenoble provides a range of transportation choices to facilitate easy navigation of the city and its environs for both locals and guests. Grenoble is easy to travel around, with reasonable and eco-friendly car rental services, beautiful bike trails, and effective public transit systems.

Public Transportation: Trams and Buses

Trams, buses, and a cable car are just a few of the effective and comprehensive public transit options offered by TAG (Transports de l'agglomération Grenobloise) in Grenoble. With many lines linking important locations including the city center, academic campuses, and residential districts, the tram network serves the city and its environs.

For commuters, students, and visitors alike, trams offer dependable and practical transportation, operating on a regular schedule throughout the day and into the evening. To make it easier to go to even the most remote parts of the city, a network of bus lines complements the tramway system, covering areas not covered by trams.

Bike Sharing and Cycling Infrastructure

Grenoble has an extensive network of bike lanes and bicycle trails that make it simple to explore the city on two wheels for tourists who are concerned about the environment and fitness lovers. Users can hire bicycles from stations spread across the city as part of the Métrovélo bike-sharing scheme. Short-term rentals and long-term subscriptions are available.

Grenoble offers bikers a safe and pleasurable way to get around while taking in the breathtaking mountain environment. In addition to bike sharing, the city has designated bike lanes and beautiful riding routes that travel through the surrounding countryside.

Car Rental and Car-Sharing Services

Grenoble provides a range of vehicle rental services and car-sharing solutions to fit every demand and budget for those who prefer the freedom and convenience of driving. It's simple to organize transportation when you arrive thanks to the presence of several foreign car rental firms with offices at the Grenoble Airport and in the city center.

Grenoble is home to car-sharing systems like Citiz and Bluely, which provide members access to a fleet of automobiles stationed across the city, in addition to regular car rental services. For quick excursions or errands where using public transit might not be feasible, these services are perfect.

Train and Bus Connections

A comprehensive network of trains and buses run by the SNCF (French National Railway Company) and regional transportation firms connects Grenoble to other French towns and areas. High-speed TGV trains to major cities like Paris, Lyon, and Marseille are available at the city's principal train station, Gare de Grenoble.

Regional TER trains are also available, catering to smaller towns and villages in the Alps and beyond.

Long-distance buses run by firms like FlixBus and Ouibus service Grenoble in addition to trains, offering reasonably priced and practical travel choices for those wishing to explore the area or go farther afield.

Grenoble has a range of transportation alternatives to meet the requirements of any tourist, whether you're seeing the French Alps by vehicle or rail, cruising around the city on a tram, or cycling along a picturesque cycle path. Grenoble's accessible, economical, and eco-friendly mobility options include an extensive bicycle infrastructure, an efficient public transportation system, and convenient vehicle rental services. These features free up your time so you can enjoy all this dynamic city and its surrounding area have to offer.

Accommodation Options

Accommodation Options in Grenoble: Finding Your Home Away from Home

Situated in the French Alps, Grenoble has an extensive array of lodging choices to accommodate every traveler's budget, inclination, and taste. Every type of tourist will find something to appreciate in this energetic city and its surroundings, from modern serviced apartments and affordable hostels to quaint boutique hotels and quaint bed & breakfasts.

Boutique Hotels: Luxurious Retreats

In the center of the city, Grenoble offers a range of boutique hotels that provide chic lodging and high-end facilities for those looking for a little more luxury and attentive care. Grenoble offers a wide selection of lodging alternatives, whether your preference is for a sleek, modern hotel with sweeping views of the Alps or a historic building with period charm.

Stay in the magnificent rooms of the Hôtel des Alpes, a boutique hotel set in a tastefully renovated 19th-century structure.

Here, you can unwind with modern furniture and indulge in fine eating at the hotel's on-site restaurant. Alternatively, get a stay at the Hôtel Le Grand Hôtel Grenoble, a stylish boutique hotel in the heart of the city, where you can rest in opulent lodging and enjoy features like a rooftop terrace, spa, and fitness center.

Bed and Breakfasts: Charming Hospitality

Staying at one of Grenoble's quaint bed and breakfasts will allow you to experience the friendliness and coziness of the French Alps. Here, you can savor handmade meals, comfortable lodging, and attentive service in a setting that seems like home. Whether you're traveling alone, with a partner, or with family and friends, bed and breakfasts provide a special chance to meet other tourists and local hosts while you explore the city and its environs.

Reserve a room at La Ferme de la Batie, a charming bed & breakfast situated in a beautifully restored farmhouse just outside of Grenoble. Here, you can take advantage of cozy lodging surrounded by verdant gardens and expansive mountain views.

Alternatively, stay at the quaint La Villa Tropezienne guesthouse, which is housed in a historic townhouse in the center of the old town. Here, you can unwind in chic rooms with retro furniture and savor a delectable breakfast that is served in the garden courtyard.

Serviced Apartments: Home Away from Home

When it comes to providing guests with the ease and comforts of home while visiting Grenoble, serviced apartments are the ideal choice. These completely furnished apartments are perfect for long-term stays or visitors seeking more space and flexibility since they provide all the facilities you need for a comfortable stay, including living spaces, private bathrooms, and kitchenettes or full kitchens.

Located in the center of Grenoble's busy Caserne de Bonne neighborhood, the Residhome Caserne de Bonne is a contemporary aparthotel offering modern amenities like a fitness center and sauna on site, spacious apartments with modern furnishings, and easy access to restaurants, shops, and public transportation. As an alternative, reserve a room at the Séjours & Affaires Marie Curie, an inexpensive aparthotel close to the university campus where you may take advantage of reasonably priced lodging that is basic but pleasant.

Budget-Friendly Hostels: Affordable Lodging

Grenoble provides a range of hostels and inexpensive housing options that offer comfortable and convenient lodging at a reasonable price for visitors on a tight budget. Hostels provide a friendly and laid-back environment where you can meet other travelers, swap travel advice, and share tales of your adventures whether you're traveling alone, with pals, or in a group.

Choose between private rooms with ensuite bathrooms and dormitory style rooms at the Auberge de Jeunesse HI Grenoble - Les Ecrins, a contemporary hostel close to the train station. Amenities include an outdoor patio, shared kitchen, and sitting area. Alternatively, reserve a room at the reasonably priced Hôtel Europole, which is situated in the heart of the city and offers basic but cozy lodging at reasonable prices along with complimentary Wi-Fi and a continental breakfast.

Grenoble has a range of lodging alternatives to fit any traveler's needs and budget, from opulent boutique hotels and quaint bed & breakfasts to contemporary serviced apartments and affordable hostels. This dynamic city and its breathtaking surroundings provide a wide range of hotel alternatives, catering to all types of travelers, romantic, family-friendly, and low-cost. So prepare to enjoy the elegance and warmth of Grenoble as you prepare your belongings, reserve your lodging, and begin your journey.

Safety Tips and Emergency Contacts

Staying Safe in Grenoble

Although Grenoble is a lively and friendly city, you should still exercise caution when visiting any metropolitan region to protect your safety and well-being. Whether you're seeing the city's historical sites, going on a hike in the nearby mountains, or savoring the regional cuisine, remembering this safety advice will make your trip to Grenoble safe and pleasurable.

General Safety Tips

Stay Aware: Pay attention to your surroundings and remain vigilant, particularly in busy places, tourist destinations, and transit hubs.

Keep Valuables Secure: Avoid flaunting valuables like jewelry, cameras, and cellphones, and always keep your possessions close to hand, especially in busy areas.

Use Licensed Taxis: When using a taxi, make sure the vehicle is licensed and owned by a respectable company. You should also always settle on the fee before you leave.

Avoid Dark or Isolated Areas: Particularly at night, stay in well-lit, crowded locations. Do not go alone in strange or secluded regions.

Stay Hydrated and Sunscreen: To avoid dehydration and sunburn when exploring outside, don't forget to apply sunscreen, remain hydrated, and shield yourself from the sun.

Emergency Contacts

During your visit to Grenoble, you may require assistance with the following critical connections, so have them on hand:

Emergency Services: To contact the police, fire department, or ambulance in an emergency, dial 112. You may call this number from any phone, including mobile phones, for no cost.

Police: You can call the local police station at 17 to report a crime or for non-emergency concerns.

Medical Emergencies: Dial 15 for all emergency medical services, including ambulance services.

Fire Department: Dial 18 in the event of a fire.

European Emergency Number: For any emergencies, including police, fire, and medical help, dial 112. This number is free to call from any phone in any of the EU's member states.

Travel Insurance

Consider acquiring travel insurance that covers unexpected occurrences such as medical crises, trip cancellations, and other travel-related expenses before departing for

Grenoble. When traveling, having travel insurance may offer financial security and peace of mind in the event of emergencies or unforeseen circumstances.

While visiting Grenoble, you can help to protect your safety and well-being by being alert to your surroundings, keeping your valuables safe, and understanding how to get emergency assistance. To ensure a safe and unforgettable visit to this stunning city tucked away in the French Alps, don't forget to prepare ahead of time, exercise caution, and take the required safety measures.

Useful Phrases in French

Gaining some practical French language skills can make your trip to Grenoble much more enjoyable. The following keywords and phrases can help you communicate efficiently while you're there:

Bonjour - Hello / Good morning
Bonsoir - Good evening
Merci - Thank you
S'il vous plaît - Please
Excusez-moi - Excuse me

Parlez-vous anglais ? - Do you speak English?

Oui - Yes

Non - No

Je ne comprends pas - I don't understand

Pouvez-vous m'aider ? - Can you help me?

Combien ça coûte ? - How much does it cost?

Où est... ? - Where is...?

Je voudrais... - I would like...

L'addition, s'il vous plaît - The bill, please

Je suis perdu(e) - I am lost

Avez-vous des recommandations ? - Do you have any recommendations?

Je suis allergique à... - I am allergic to...

Pouvez-vous répéter, s'il vous plaît ? - Can you repeat, please?

Je suis désolé(e) - I'm sorry

Bonne journée ! - Have a good day!

By using these expressions regularly, you'll not only be able to connect with Grenoble residents more easily but also demonstrate your attempt to speak their language, which is frequently welcomed.

Additional Resources

Further Reading and Websites

Here are some suggested websites and resources for more reading, details about Grenoble's attractions and activities, and useful travel advice:

Grenoble Tourism Official Website: Grenoble's official tourist website provides a wealth of information about the city's activities, transit choices, lodging, and attractions. Maps, itineraries, and planning advice are also available.

Grenoble Tourism Official Website

Lonely Planet - Grenoble: Grenoble is one of the locations covered by Lonely Planet, which offers comprehensive travel advice and recommendations for all of the world's places. In addition to useful travel tips, their website provides insights into the city's history, culture, and attractions.

Lonely Planet - Grenoble

TripAdvisor - Grenoble: TripAdvisor provides opinions and suggestions from visitors to Grenoble on accommodations, dining options, tourist sites, and other topics. Utilizing the internet, you may arrange your schedule and find the city's hidden treasures.

TripAdvisor - Grenoble

The Culture Trip - Grenoble: The Culture Trip offers guides, articles, and information about Grenoble's cultural sites and activities. To make your trip to the city more enjoyable, you may discover information on local events, local art, music, and food.

A Cultural Journey to Grenoble

French Moments - Grenoble: This website provides information and guides on a range of French locations, including Grenoble. Through their educational material, you may discover more about the history, monuments, and culture of the city.

French Moments - Grenoble

These websites will provide you with insightful knowledge and useful advice to help you organize and maximize your vacation to Grenoble. This little Alpine community has enough to offer everyone, whether they like cultural events, outdoor pursuits, or delicious cuisine.

Maps and Apps for Exploring Grenoble

Several maps and applications are quite useful for getting around and enjoying Grenoble. Here are a few suggested choices: **Google Maps:** Offering comprehensive maps, directions, and real-time navigation, Google Maps is a dependable and adaptable mapping application. It allows you to plan your trips whether you're driving, walking, or taking public transit, as well as to explore the streets of Grenoble and locate hotels, restaurants, and attractions. Additionally, the app has offline maps, which is useful if you're traveling through places with spotty internet access.

Google Maps - Grenoble

Maps.me: You may download comprehensive maps of Grenoble and use them to navigate without an internet connection with our free offline mapping tool. With its ability to give details about hotels, restaurants, and other establishments, the app is a helpful resource for city exploration by bike or foot. Maps.me - Grenoble

Citymapper: Citymapper is a transit app that offers up-to-date details about Grenoble's public transportation alternatives, including buses, trams, and cable cars. The app makes it easy to plan your trips, look up timetables, and get real-time notifications regarding delays and disturbances, so your commute across the city runs smoothly and efficiently. Citymapper - Grenoble

Grenoble City Pass App: If you've bought a Grenoble City Pass, you may access details on discounted tickets, exclusive deals, and featured attractions by downloading the official app. The app lets you make the most of your trip to the city by helping you arrange your schedule and find hidden treasures. Grenoble City Pass App

VéloMagg: The VéloMagg app offers details on the city's bike-sharing system, such as station locations, bike availability, and rental instructions, if you're going to explore Grenoble on two wheels. It's simple to travel around on two wheels with the help of the app, which lets you pay for your trips, unlock bikes, and locate the closest bike station.

VéloMagg - Grenoble

Whether you're touring Grenoble's historic monuments, figuring out the public transit system, or finding hidden treasures off the main route, these maps and apps will make your travels easier. With these resources at your disposal, you'll be ready to take full advantage of your trip to this enchanting Alpine city.

Tourist Information Centers

The tourist information offices in the city of Grenoble provide helpful advice and useful information. The following Grenoble tourist information offices are suggested:

Grenoble Tourist Office - Place Victor Hugo: Situated in Place Victor Hugo in the city center, the Grenoble Tourist Office provides a comprehensive array of services to assist guests in making the most of their trip. Maps, pamphlets, and details on sights, activities, lodging, and travel alternatives are available. In addition, the competent staff is on hand to address any inquiries and offer tailored suggestions for your stay.

Address: Victor Hugo Place, Grenoble, France, 38000

Website: Grenoble Tourist Office

Grenoble Alpes Métropole Tourist Office - **Grenoble Gare:** Travelers arriving in the city by train may get help and information from the Grenoble Alpes Métropole Tourist Office, which is conveniently located close to the train station. You may pick up tourist passes, maps, and guides there, and you can also find information about local lodging, transportation, and activities. You may schedule trips and activities and create an itinerary with the assistance of the staff.

Address: 7 Place de la Gare, 38000 Grenoble, France

Website: Grenoble Alpes Métropole Tourist Office

Grenoble Tourist Information Point - Grenoble Airport: If you're traveling by plane to Grenoble, you may get help and information about the city and its surroundings by going to the Tourist Information Point at Grenoble Airport. The helpful staff can assist you with making reservations for lodging and activities during your visit, as well as providing you with maps, brochures, and information on transit alternatives.

Address: Grenoble Alpes Isère Airport, 38590 Saint-Étienne-de-Saint-Geoirs, France

Website: Grenoble Alpes Isère Airport

When it comes to helping tourists make the most of their time in this quaint Alpine city, these tourist information centers are a great source of advice, information, and support. These centers' staff are committed to making your stay in Grenoble unique and pleasurable, whether you require assistance with itinerary planning, lodging reservations, or navigating the city's transit choices.

Conclusion

Saying Goodbye to Thailand Grenoble

It might be difficult to say goodbye to Grenoble, but you will always have fond recollections of your travels, discoveries, and adventures there. Here are a few closing reflections and suggestions to treasure as you say goodbye to this enchanting city:

Final Thoughts:

Gratitude for Memories: Think back for a minute on the amazing experiences you had while visiting Grenoble. Cherish these moments and keep them near to your heart, whether you're experiencing the natural beauty of the Alps, indulging in delectable food, or touring ancient sites.

Connection with Locals: You will probably never forget the friendliness and kindness of everyone you have encountered in Grenoble. The relationships you've formed, whether through a casual conversation with a neighborhood store owner or over lunch with recently made friends, have enhanced your experience and given your adventure more dimension.

Appreciation for Culture: Numerous chances for exploration and discovery have been made possible by Grenoble's dynamic culture and rich history. You have experienced this fascinating city's diverse culture, from its museums and galleries to its exciting festivals and events.

Recommendations:

Keepsakes and Souvenirs: You might want to get a few souvenirs to help you remember your time in Grenoble. These treasures, which might be anything from a jar of handmade jam to a piece of locally created artwork, will act as mementos of your incredible travels.

Stay Connected: Remain in contact with the people you met and the locations you experienced while in Grenoble. Get newsletters, follow neighborhood companies and associations on social media, and keep up with events and goings-on in the city. You never know when life will bring you together again.

Plan Your Return: Even though leaving Grenoble may be tough, remember that it's only a temporary farewell. Begin daydreaming and organizing your next visit to this fascinating city and the breathtaking Alps that are around it. Grenoble will be there to greet you with open arms when you return, whether that be in ten years or next year.

Take with you the memories, relationships, and experiences that have influenced your path as you bid Grenoble farewell. And never forget that even if your time in Grenoble is coming to an end, your passion for exploration and adventure will never die. Goodbye, Grenoble, till we cross paths once more.

Printed in Dunstable, United Kingdom